SCIENCE THROUGH Art

Water

Hilary Devonshire

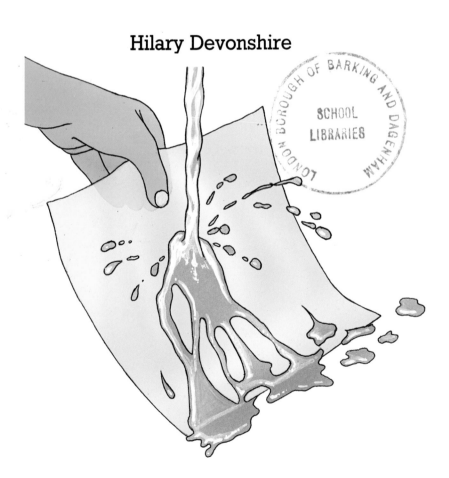

FRANKLIN WATTS

London/New York/Sydney/Toronto

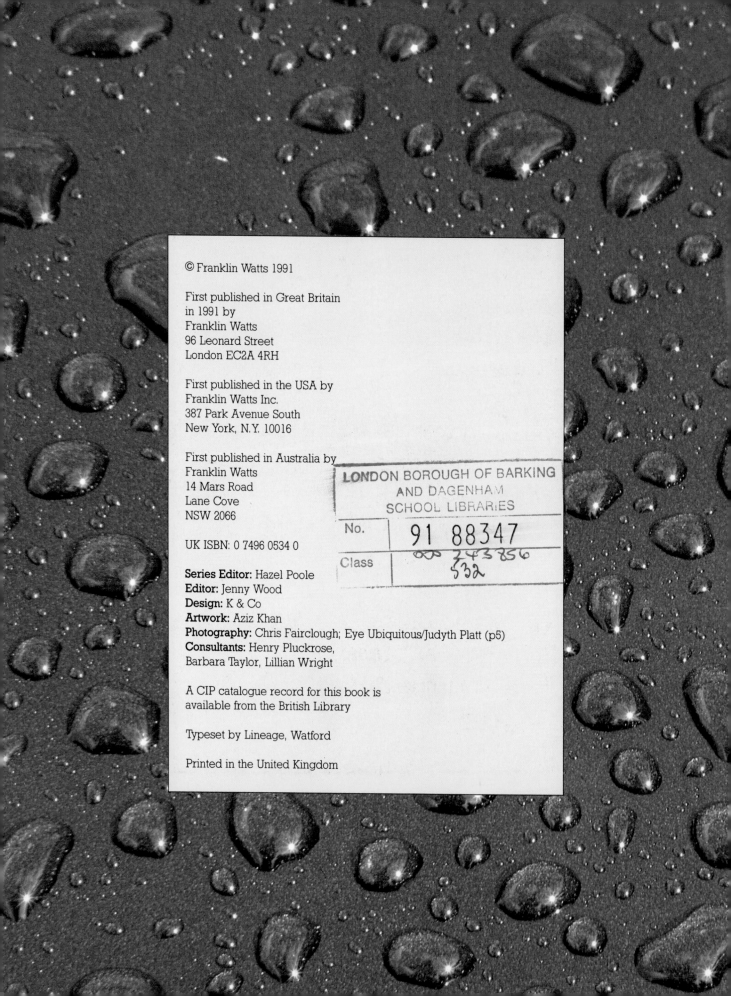

© Franklin Watts 1991

First published in Great Britain
in 1991 by
Franklin Watts
96 Leonard Street
London EC2A 4RH

First published in the USA by
Franklin Watts Inc.
387 Park Avenue South
New York, N.Y. 10016

First published in Australia by
Franklin Watts
14 Mars Road
Lane Cove
NSW 2066

UK ISBN: 0 7496 0534 0

Series Editor: Hazel Poole
Editor: Jenny Wood
Design: K & Co
Artwork: Aziz Khan
Photography: Chris Fairclough; Eye Ubiquitous/Judyth Platt (p5)
Consultants: Henry Pluckrose,
Barbara Taylor, Lillian Wright

A CIP catalogue record for this book is
available from the British Library

Typeset by Lineage, Watford

Printed in the United Kingdom

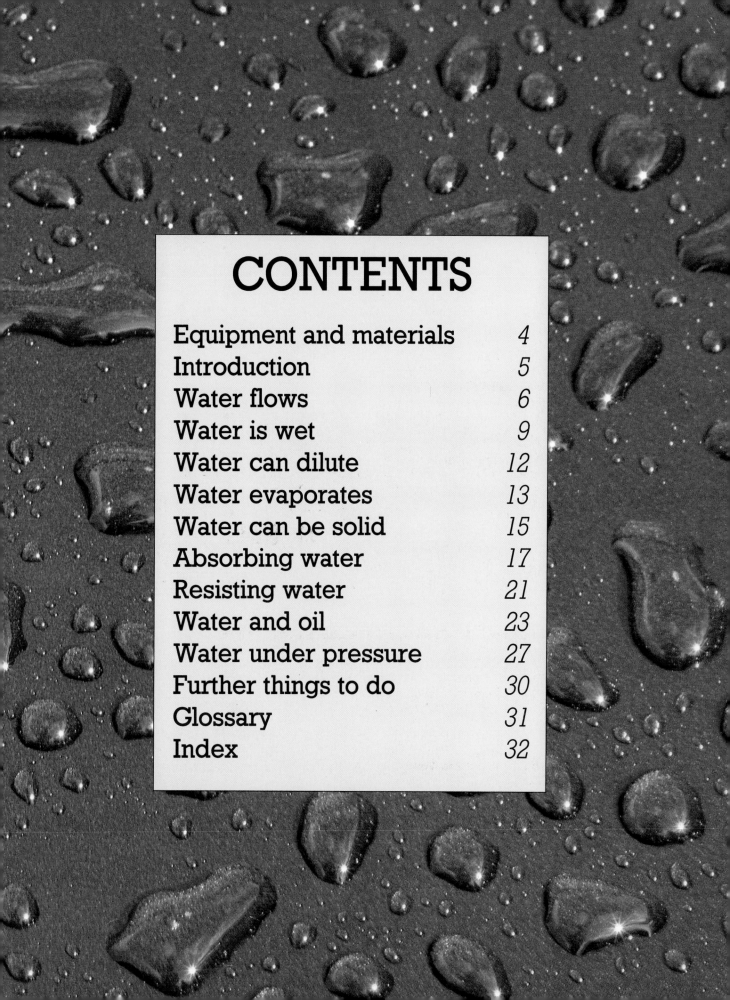

CONTENTS

EQUIPMENT AND MATERIALS

This book describes activities which use the following:

Aluminium foil
Baking tray
Board (chopping board or artist's
    cutting board)
Bowl
Card (thin)
Cold water dyes
Cooking oil
Craft knife
Diffuser spray
Drinking straws
Dropper
Felt-tip pens (water-based)
Glue (acrylic PVA)
Ink – Indian
    – marbling inks in various colours
    – various coloured inks
Jam jars
Jar with screw-top lid
Kitchen towels
Linseed oil
Liquid detergent
Magnifying glass
Modelling clay
Newspaper
Paint – oil
    – powder
    – water colour

Paintbrushes
Paper – black paper
    – blotting paper
    – cartridge paper
    – coffee filter paper
    – sugar paper
    – tissue paper
    – white paper for drawing on
Pen
Pencil
Ruler (metal)
Salt
Scissors
Serviettes (white paper)
Spoon
Stapler
Stick
Thread
Water

INTRODUCTION

Water covers over 70% of the Earth's surface and is probably the world's most useful substance. Every living thing needs water in order to survive.

Water is interesting because it is a liquid. It is colourless, odourless and tasteless.

By following the investigations in this book, you will learn something about the science of water and also about the nature of liquids. At the start of each section there are some scientific ideas to be explored. A scientist looks at ideas and tries to discover if they are always true, and will also investigate to see if they can be disproved. You will be working like a scientist. A scientist is curious and wants to find out about the world in which we live. A scientist tests ideas, makes investigations and experiments, and tries to explain what has happened. Your results may be surprising or unexpected, and then you will find that you need to make a new investigation or test a new idea.

You will also be an artist. You will be using water in the art activities which are included in each section. Through working with both water and the various art materials and techniques, you will make discoveries about how water behaves and how water can be used. Your finished pieces of art will be a record of your scientific findings.

WATER FLOWS

Water always flows downwards, because of an invisible force called gravity which pulls everything towards the centre of the Earth. When water cannot go down any further, it settles at the lowest level it can find. If the surface on which it settles is completely flat, the water will not flow.

Gravity makes water flow downwards.

Water will not flow if it settles on a completely flat surface.

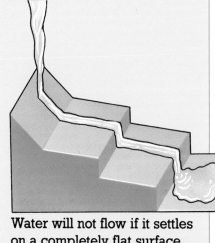

If a drop of water falls on a flat surface it will not flow on its own.

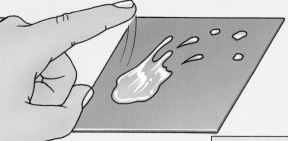

Water can be made to move if it is blown on or pushed.

Watch rainwater flowing in the gutter. Which way does it flow? Where else can you see water flow?

Crumpled paper art

You will need: several sheets of paper, bowls or jars of water, coloured inks, a dropper and a straw.

1 Crumple a sheet of paper, then unfold it so that it makes a paper "bowl". The creases in the paper are the channels down which the water will flow. Colour the water in one of the bowls or jars by adding a few drops of ink. This will allow you to see the flowing water clearly.

2 Fold in a rim about 2.5cm (1 inch) wide right round the top edge of your paper "bowl".

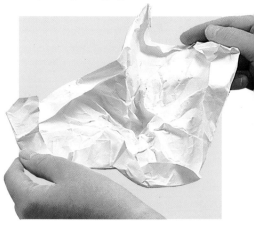

3 Fill a dropper or straw with some of the coloured water, then release a few drops around your paper bowl. Drop the water close to the rim, on the inside of the bowl. Watch where the water flows.

4 Once the water has reached the lowest parts of the channels, it may settle in small pools at the bottom. You can make a channel on the rim to pour away the extra water. Leave the paper to dry.

5 You can mount your crumpled picture on card.

6 ... or you can iron out the creases with a warm iron. Notice how the coloured water creates an interesting pattern in the channels.

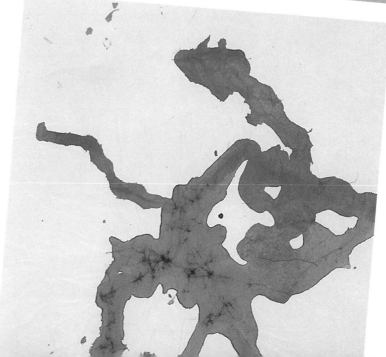

Smudge Print

You will need: a sheet of paper, coloured inks, a dropper or a straw.

1 Fold a sheet of paper in half, then open it out. Drop a few drops of different coloured inks along the fold. You need only one or two drops of each colour. How can you make the ink move?

2 Fold the paper in half again. With one finger, and working from the fold out towards the edges of the paper, gently press the surface. What happens to the ink? Unfold the paper and look at your finished design. It is symmetrical – one side is exactly the same as the other.

Water on a flat surface

You will need: paper, coloured inks, a dropper and a straw.

1 Release one drop of coloured water on to another sheet of paper, then blow gently through the straw on to the water drop. What is making the water move outwards? Make another design using several different colours of ink.

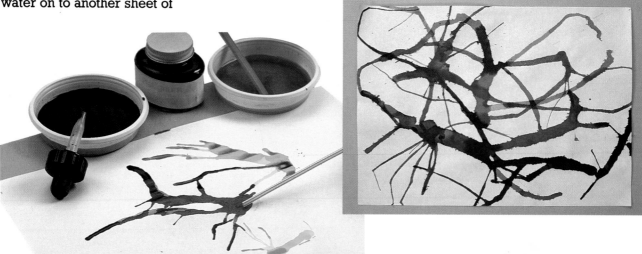

WATER IS WET

Water can make dry things wet. Objects can be made damp or wet by dipping them in water. Water can be added to substances such as dry powder colour to form a solution. The water acts as a solvent for the other substance.

Dry powder and water mix to form a solution.

Objects when dipped in, or covered with water become damp or wet.

When you have a bath or shower you get wet all over. What does it feel like when you walk in the rain?

Wet and Dry

You will need: water, powder paint, paper, paintbrushes.

1 Mix some dry powder colour with water to make wet paint.

2 Sprinkle dry powder colour on to wet paper.

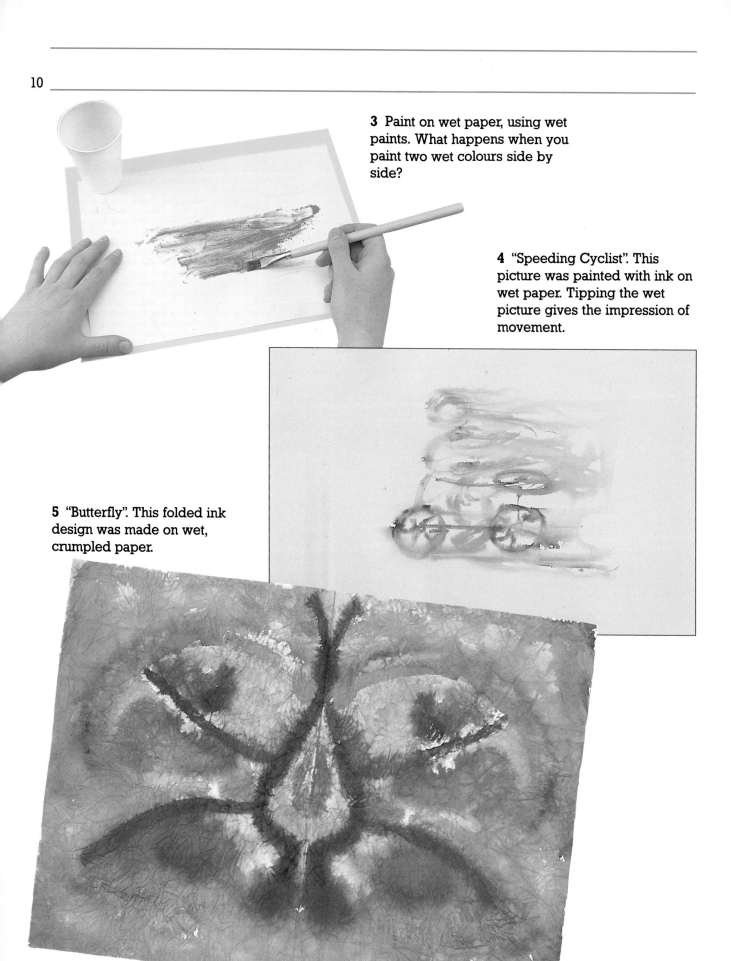

3 Paint on wet paper, using wet paints. What happens when you paint two wet colours side by side?

4 "Speeding Cyclist". This picture was painted with ink on wet paper. Tipping the wet picture gives the impression of movement.

5 "Butterfly". This folded ink design was made on wet, crumpled paper.

A wet circle

A pulling force called surface tension works on the surface of a liquid, which makes it seem as if it has an elastic skin. This stops it from spreading out over a wider area.

You will need: a sheet of paper, water, a large paintbrush, coloured inks, a dropper or a straw.

1 Using a large brush, paint a circle of water on a dry piece of paper. Drop a little coloured ink on to the wet circle. Watch the colours blend together and flow out towards the edge of the circle. What happens when the colours reach the edge of the circle? Why do you think this is?

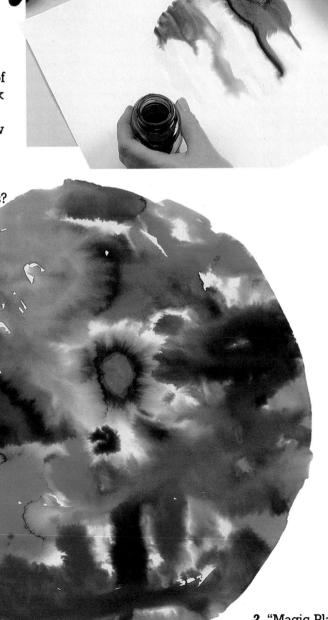

2 "Magic Planet". What happens if you begin with a wet square or a wet triangle?

WATER CAN DILUTE

Water can be added to other liquids to dilute them, that is, to reduce their strength. In art, the strength of water soluble colours, for example, paints, dyes and inks, can be diluted (made weaker) by adding water. The water is the solvent.

Concentrated fruit drinks need to be diluted with water before you drink them.

Can you think of any other substances which are diluted with water before they are used?

Adding water to another liquid dilutes the liquid.

Making a Colour Chart

You will need: powder paints, jars or bowls of water, a paintbrush and paper.

1 Add water to some powder paint. Start by making a strong, thick paint, then gradually add water....

.... Make a chart to show how the colour changes as you dilute the paint. Notice how the strength of the colour becomes weaker and the paint becomes paler in tone.

"A red colour chart"

Can you make a chart in reverse by gradually adding more powder colour to very dilute watery paint?

Painting with water-colours

When you paint with water-colours, you do not need to add white paint. The paler colours are made by dilution with water.

"Water-colour landscape"

WATER EVAPORATES

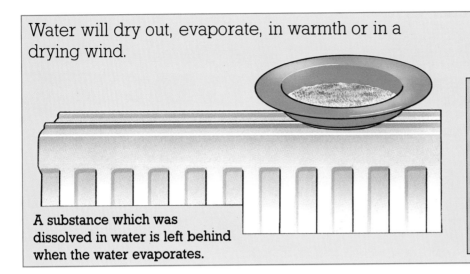

Water will dry out, evaporate, in warmth or in a drying wind.

A substance which was dissolved in water is left behind when the water evaporates.

Have you watched washing blowing in the wind? The water evaporates and the clothes dry quickly.

When you dry your hair with a hairdryer, the warm moving air causes the water to evaporate.

Making salt crystals

You will need: a glass jar (or a pan), a spoon, hot water, salt, thread, a short stick or old pencil, modelling clay, black paper, a light scope or magnifying glass, a pencil and a sheet of white paper.

1 Ask an adult to help you with this part of the experiment. Carefully pour some hot water into the jar or pan. If you use a glass jar, place a spoon in the jar before pouring in the water to prevent the glass from cracking. Once the water is safely in the jar, remove the spoon. Add salt a little at a time, and watch the salt dissolve in the hot water. Continue to add salt until the water has dissolved all the salt it can and some remains at the bottom of the jar. You now have a saturated salt-water solution.

2 Tie a length of thread to the stick or old pencil, then put a little modelling clay on the other end as a weight. Hang the thread in the saturated salt solution for a few days.

3 Watch for salt crystals to form as the water evaporates.

4 Place some of the crystals on the black paper .... and study them through the light scope or magnifying glass. You could also use a microscope to observe your crystals closely. What shape are the crystals?

5 Use a soft drawing pencil to make a sketch of what you see.

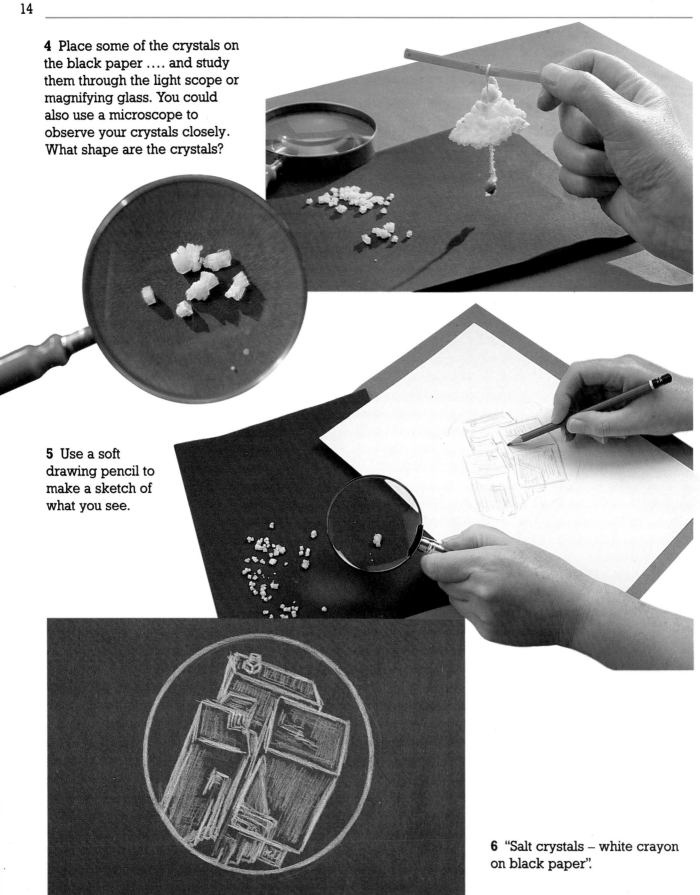

6 "Salt crystals – white crayon on black paper".

WATER CAN BE SOLID

When water freezes and turns from a liquid into a solid, it becomes snow or ice. Snow is made up of tiny crystals, each of which usually has six sides.

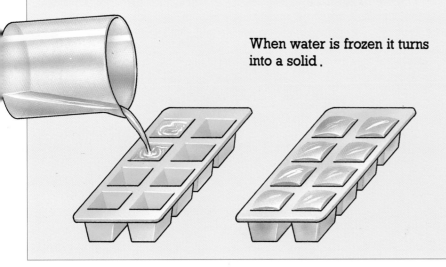

When water is frozen it turns into a solid.

Have you tried to catch a snowflake? They melt very quickly in warm hands so are difficult to study closely.

When water turns to ice, it expands. This is why ice is less dense and therefore lighter than water, why ice cubes float in a drink and why icebergs float in the sea.

A snow-crystal design

You will need: a small piece of card, a pen or pencil, a ruler, scissors, paper (white and black) and glue.

Like the salt in the last experiment, water in its solid form, snow, is made up of tiny crystals. Each snowflake is a cluster of hexagonal ice crystals.

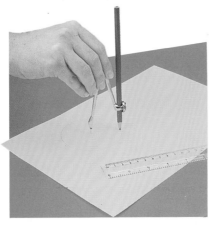

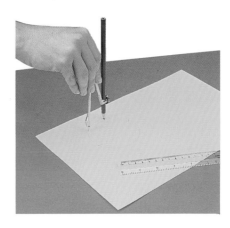

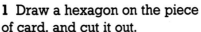

1 Draw a hexagon on the piece of card, and cut it out.

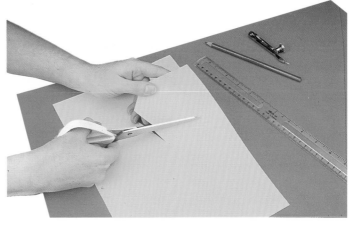

2 Using the hexagon as a template, draw some hexagons on the white paper. You will need about 8.

3 Cut out the hexagons you have drawn.

4 Fold each hexagon three times as shown. Cut small pieces from the edges of each folded hexagon.

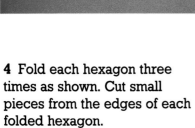

5 Carefully unfold the cut shapes and glue them on to the black paper to make a snow crystal design.

Like snow crystals, each hexagonal pattern is unique.

ABSORBING WATER

Different materials, such as blotting paper, soak up, or absorb, water at different rates.

Some materials absorb water very easily.

After you've washed your hands, you use an absorbent towel to dry them. What might the towel be made of?

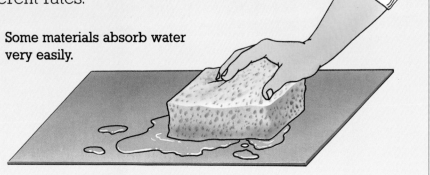

Absorbency Test I

You will need: newspaper, a selection of paper types (e.g. thick/thin, rough/smooth, shiny/dull), a drinking straw or dropper, water, coloured inks, paper clip/sellotape, a short stick, a bowl and water based felt-tip pens.

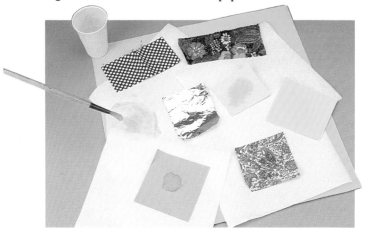

1 Prepare a selection of small squares from your paper samples.

2 Cover your work surface with a thick layer of newspaper. Using the dropper or straw, drop a blob of water on to the surface of each square. Notice what happens to the blobs. Which papers absorb the water most easily?

Absorbency Test II

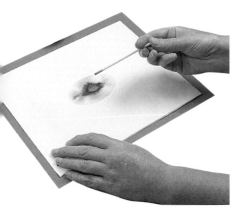

1 Choose a paper which absorbs the water easily. Drop a spot of coloured ink on to the paper and watch it spread. What happens if you drop a second colour on to the centre of the same spot? Try adding more colours. Watch what happens.

2 Try again, starting with two spots a little way (6 cm/2½″) apart. Compare your results.

"Circular design. Inks on blotting paper".

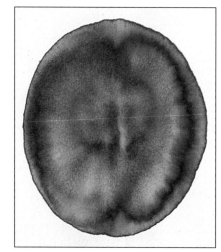

Chromotography

You will need: a very absorbent paper such as a filter paper, kitchen towel or blotting paper, a short stick, coloured inks, water-based felt-tip pens, a bowl and water.

1 Cut pieces of very absorbent paper into strips. Attach the strips to the stick. Make an ink spot on each strip.

2 Pour some water into the bottom of the bowl. Lay the stick across the bowl so that the strips of paper just touch the surface of the water.

3 Watch the water soak along the paper. The water acts as a solvent, carrying the coloured ink with it.

Repeat this experiment using different makes and colours of ink. Try using water-based felt-tip pens, too. Make all your ink spots a similar size, and compare the strips that are produced. What do you notice?

Paper tie-and-dye

You will need: cold water dyes, water, white paper serviettes and a pair of old rubber gloves.

1 Prepare a small quantity of different coloured cold-water dyes.

2 Fold a number of white paper serviettes in different ways....

Fan folds
Twists
Diagonal folds
Straight folds

3 Dip one end of the folded serviette into a dye. Lift it up quickly so that only a little dye is absorbed. Repeat by dipping the other end, then the middle, into other colours. Leave to dry.

4 Gently unfold the serviette to see the pattern. Do not unfold it before it is dry or it will tear. You can use a warm iron to speed up the drying process.

5 Some interesting tie-and-dye patterns. Can you tell which pattern was made with a concertina fold?

RESISTING WATER

Materials which do not soak up water at all are waterproof. They resist water. It is possible to make materials which soak up water waterproof, too, by covering them with a coating of wax, oil or plastic.

When it rains we use umbrellas, raincoats and boots to keep dry. Have a look at the clothes you wear in the rain. What materials have been used to make them?

Some materials resist water.

These materials are waterproof. They keep water out.

Waterproof Tests

You will need: different types of paper, water, PVA glue and a paintbrush.

1 Try the absorbency test (see page 17) with squares of plastic, greaseproof paper, kitchen foil and waterproof fabric. How water resistant are they?

2 Brush some PVA glue on to a piece of paper and leave to dry. Now brush water over the paper. What do you notice?

Waterproof Pictures

You will need: PVA glue, paper,
paintbrushes, Indian ink,
coloured ink and water.

1 Use diluted PVA glue to draw
a picture on white paper. Leave
to dry. Paint an ink wash over
the picture. The glue will resist
the ink.

2 Draw a picture on a sheet of
white paper, using black Indian
ink. Leave to dry.

3 Paint a coloured ink wash
over the whole picture. The
lines already drawn in India ink
will resist the ink wash.

WATER AND OIL

Some substances do not dissolve in water. Oil is a good example. It will not mix with water. Instead, oil floats on the surface because it is less dense, or "lighter" than water.

Oil is less dense than water, so it floats on the surface.

Have you seen ducks shaking water from their feathers? The ducks' feathers are oily. How does the oil on their feathers help them to stay afloat?

Sometimes oil is spilt into the sea from a ship. Because oil floats on water, floating booms are used to stop the oil from spreading. It can then be skimmed or pumped from the surface. Detergents can also be used to break down the oil.

Some experiments with oil and water

You will need: a screw-top jar filled with water, and cooking oil.

1 Add a little cooking oil to the water in the screw-top jar. Watch what happens.

2 Screw the lid on tightly and shake the jar. What happens?

Patterns with marbling inks

You will need: a tray, water, marbling inks, drinking straws, paper and liquid detergent.

1 Drop a little of the marbling inks on to the surface of some water in the tray. Why do you think they float on the surface?

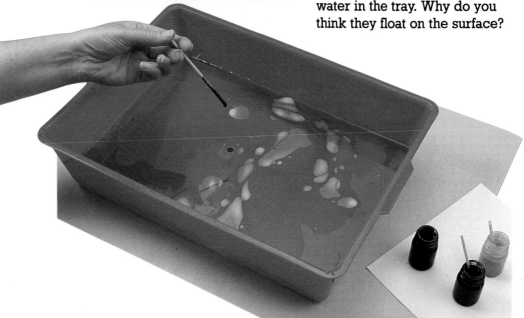

2 Using a straw, gently swirl the colours into a pattern.

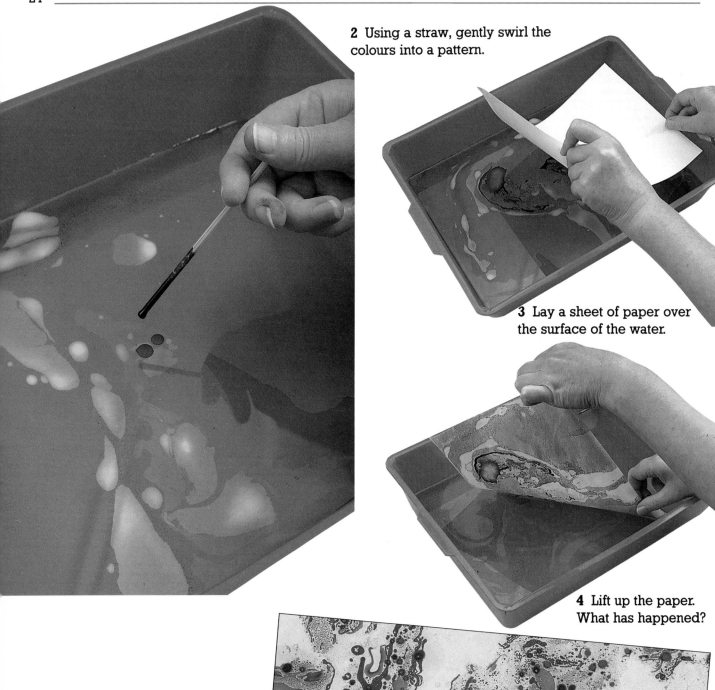

3 Lay a sheet of paper over the surface of the water.

4 Lift up the paper. What has happened?

Repeat this activity once more, but this time add a tiny drop of very diluted liquid detergent to the water after you have added the marbling inks. What happens to your design? Can you explain why this is?

An experiment with oil paints and water-colours

You will need: oil paint, linseed oil, water-colour paint, paper, scissors and glue.

1 Dilute some oil paint with a little linseed oil, to make it runny. Drop a little of the diluted oil paint and some water-colour on to a folded sheet of paper.

2 Fold the paper over the colours.... and press gently.

3 Unfold the paper and examine the print. Interesting patterns have been made because the oil paint and water-colours will not mix. Study your patterns. You may find some which remind you of a landscape with water reflections.

4 Cut out some of the patterns and glue them on to a colourful background to make a collage.

WATER UNDER PRESSURE

If water is pushed, it flows more quickly. Forcing water out of a small hole under pressure creates a powerful jet which travels at high speed. If the hole is very small, the water will be pushed apart and come out in a fine spray. This is called diffusion.

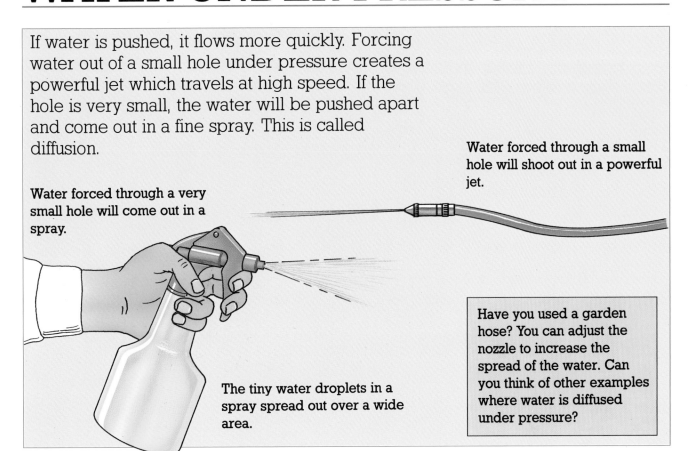

Water forced through a very small hole will come out in a spray.

Water forced through a small hole will shoot out in a powerful jet.

The tiny water droplets in a spray spread out over a wide area.

Have you used a garden hose? You can adjust the nozzle to increase the spread of the water. Can you think of other examples where water is diffused under pressure?

Spray pictures

You will need: a piece of thin card, a pencil, a craft knife, a board (such as a chopping board or artist's cutting board), a metal ruler, a diffuser spray, coloured ink, tape and newspaper.

1 Draw a shape on the piece of thin card. Carefully, cut out the shape, using the craft knife.

2 Lift the cut shape out of the card.

3 Keep the piece of card from which the shape has been cut. This piece of card is a stencil.

4 Fix the cut-out shape against a vertical sheet of paper. You will need to protect the background support and floor with newspaper. Using the diffuser, experiment by spraying ink (a water-based liquid) around the edges of the shape.

5 Remove the card shape.
What do you notice?

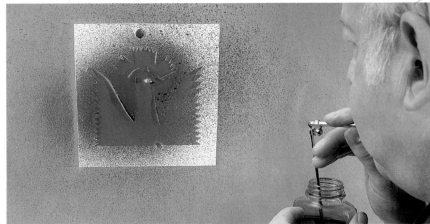

6 Repeat the experiment using
the stencil. Spray the ink into
the space left by the shape.

7 Compare the two pictures.
How do they differ?

FURTHER THINGS TO DO

Papier-Mâché

Because newspaper is very absorbent, it is a good material to use for papier-mâché.

A glove puppet

1 Mix a small amount of wallpaper paste in a bowl. Tear some newspaper into small pieces and drop them into the paste. Stir well.

2 If the mixture is too stiff, add a little more water.

3 The mixture needs to be stiff enough to mould into a ball shape. This will form the head.

4 Make a tube of thin card to fit over your finger. Push this tube halfway into the head and then shape the features on the puppet's face. When the head is dry, paint the face. Attach the clothes to the tube with PVA glue.

"Papier-mâché creature"

An illustrated dictionary

Make an illustrated dictionary of words which have links with water, such as water-boatman, watercress, waterfall, water-wheel.

A photographic study

Use a camera to take photographs of how water is used in our world. You can begin by using the ideas mentioned in each section of this book.

Painting on fabric

Using watery paints, inks or dyes, paint a picture on a piece of cotton fabric. Watch how the colours are absorbed.

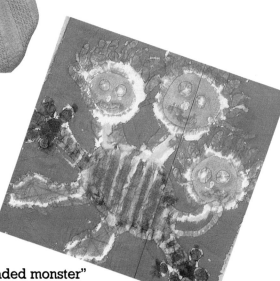

"Three headed monster"

GLOSSARY

Absorb
To soak up. Some materials absorb water easily.

Chromotography
A way of separating different colours.

Crystals
Solids made up of particles called molecules which are linked together in regular, geometric patterns. Salt crystals are cube shaped, while snow crystals are hexagonal.

Diffusion
Dispersal of liquid in small droplets from one point.

Dilute
To make a solution less strong by adding water.

Dissolve
To become part of a solution. For example, sugar dissolves in water to become a sugar solution.

Dry
Opposite to wet. No moisture.

Evaporation
A drying process in which a liquid becomes a gas, through heat or drying wind.

Float
To rest on the surface of a liquid, for example, oil will float on water.

Flow
To move easily. The force of gravity will always cause water to flow downwards.

Gas
A substance which has no shape. It can fill all the space inside any container.

Liquid
Not a solid, nor a gas, but a runny substance, which can flow. A liquid will take on the shape of any container into which it is poured.

Particle
A tiny piece.

Pressure
A force on a given area.

Resist
To keep out. Materials which resist water do not allow water to be absorbed.

Saturate
To absorb the maximum quantity. A saturated salt water solution will not allow any more salt to be absorbed.

Solid
A hard shape, not a liquid. A solid keeps its shape.

Solution
Substances — for example, sugar or salt — can be dissolved in water to make a solution. The water is the solvent.

Solvent
A substance, such as water, which is able to dissolve or form a solution with another substance. Water is a good solvent and is used to make many solutions.

Surface tension
A pulling force on the surface of a liquid, like an invisible elastic skin, which stops it spreading out over a wider area.

Water
A colourless, odourless, tasteless liquid. Water is found in all living matter and is necessary for life.

Waterproof
Waterproof materials resist water and stop it soaking in.

Wet
Opposite to dry. Moist with water.